PERKINS FAMILY HISTORY

European Royalty to West Tennessee

By

Katherine Fletcher

INTRODUCTION

This particular Perkins family line goes back an amazing forty nine generations.   My   humble family line from West Tennessee who were small farmers actually came from ancient Kings and Queens of France and England.   Follow the journey from the year 600 AD and this family's journey from Germany, France, England and America.

This American branch settled in Jamestown, VA and Baltimore, Maryland.   Some lived in Bladen, North Carolina and parts of South Carolina and Washington and Carter Counties in Tennessee.   My branch lived in Hardin County (Sardis), Tennessee.

PERKINS FAMILY HISTORY

Perkins is one of the most notable surnames from the European genealogical research of Anglo/Saxon surnames, and is an influential surname of the middle ages.   It should be noted at the beginning that the original spelling of the name was not Perkins.   The name was originally deMorlaix as the manuscripts of this time period were, most always, written in Latin or French.   The later translators Anglicized the name from deMorlaix to Morley. In future generations the Perkins (deMorlaix/Morley) name was spelt Pierrekin, Pierkyn, and Perkyn. Not until the late 14th century did the spelling take on the now accepted form.

Research of ancient manuscripts, which include the Doomsday Book by Duke William of Normandy in 1086 A.D., the Ragman Rolls of 1291-1296 authorized by King Edward 1st of England, the Curia Regis Rolls, The Pipe Rolls and The Hearth Rolls of England, found the first record of the name Perkins in Leicestershire, England.   The name Perkins, in one form or another (i.e.: deMorlaix/Morley), first appears on the census rolls taken by the Kings of England beginning about 400 A.D.

The family name Perkins is one of the most distinguished of the ancient world during a time of Kingdoms, Kings and Knights.   If we are to believe Bede, the Chronicler of the Saxons, this founding race of England was led by the Saxon General/Commanders Hengist and Horsa and settled in Kent.

However, there is evidence to support the claim that the name is of Celtic/Welsh origin.   Based on British history we know that after the last Roman Legions left the continent in the early part of the 5th century the Saxons, Angles and other LowGerman tribes settled in Southeastern England around Kent.   However, the Ancient Britons (Celtics) were the true natives of the area and it is an amalgamation of the Angles, Saxons and Celtic Britons who became what we refer to today as the Anglo/Saxons.   The truth is that the Angles and Saxons may have "moved in", but the Britons were there in far greater numbers, thus accounting for the claim that the blood line is far more Celtic than any other.   Therefore it should be concluded that the origins of the Perkins "Clan" are Celtic/Welsh.

By the 13th century the family name Perkins emerged as a notable English family in the county of Leicester, where they were recorded as a family of great antiquity seated as Lords of the manor and estates in that shire.   They had branched to Ufton Court in Berkshire and Sutton Coldfield in Warwickshire, later branching to Nuneaton, Marston and Hillmorton, Warwickshire.   The main stem of the family continued at Orton Hall in Leicestershire, where it remains to this day. Notable amongst the family at this time was Perkins of Leicester.   For the next two or three centuries bearers of the surname Perkins flourished and played a significant role in the political development of England.

The last generation to use the original spelling of Morlaix in or around 1331 was the family of one Pierre de Morlaix of Shropshire, England. He appears to have been born 1312 in Bretagne, Morliax, Normandy, France and died about 1384 in Shropshire, England. His name indicates that although originally from Morlaix, Normandy, France he was part of the Celtic/Welsh group previously mentioned who migrated to England. During this time period surnames were not in common use. Everybody was known by some personal characteristic such as what they did, who there father was or where they came from, hence Pierre de Morlaix was from Morlaix, France. Attaining a high position within English society, Pierre became the High Steward of the Hugo de Spencer Estate of Oxfordshire, England (later known as the House of Spencer, of whom Princes Diana was a daughter).

The Perkins of Ufton, Berkshire, are generally believed by genealogists to be the parent branch from which nearly all the Perkins of England and America are descended.

From William Perkins (1495), of Hillmorton Parish, Warwickshire, was descended the John Perkins who possibly was the one that settled in Ipswich, MA and was the progenitor of many American branches of the Perkins Family.

GENERATION ONE

Zona Louise Perkins (1887-1959) and Charles Walter Rice (1886-1973)

They married in 1904.   Zona ran the post office for many years. Charles Walter (my great grandfather) was an excellent carpenter.   I have an heirloom hand made cedar chest that he made for my mother when she got married.   Walter and Zona ran the first telephone company in Sardis for many years.

Sardis, Tennessee

Their children:

Rupert Kerry Rice   1913-1923 died of ruptured appendix at age 12

Mildred Nellie 1919-1919 died as a baby of cholera

Howard 1912-

Oral Holland   (my grandfather) 1912-1993/ married Margaret Ruth England

Millie Lucille "Lucy" Rice   1925 - married Paul Everette Martin

Paul (1921-1991) married Mildred Martin

** THE RICE GENEALOGY IS ALSO COMPLETED AND AVAILABLE ON AMAZON.

Here's some great pictures of Zona Perkins and her boys and husband.

Charles Walter Rice

GENERATION TWO

Charles (Mack) Perkins (1860-1936) and Lydia A. Hopper (1862-1936)

In 1880 they lived in Henderson, TN age 19.

Born in Henderson, Tennessee - died in Decatur Co, TN.

Lydia Hopper's parents are David Crockett Hopper and Martha Ann Pearly Bridges.

Their children:

Emma 1879-1970 married Luther Wilmer Johnson

Thomas Valentine 1883-1937 / married Ida Bivens

Willie Paul 1898-1980 married Vida Kennedy

Robert 1887-

Zona 1887-1959   she died of pellagra

Jesse   1891-

He divorced Lydia before 1900 and He also married in 1908 to Betty J. Tipton and had children:

Frank J.

Opal Flossie   1911-1992

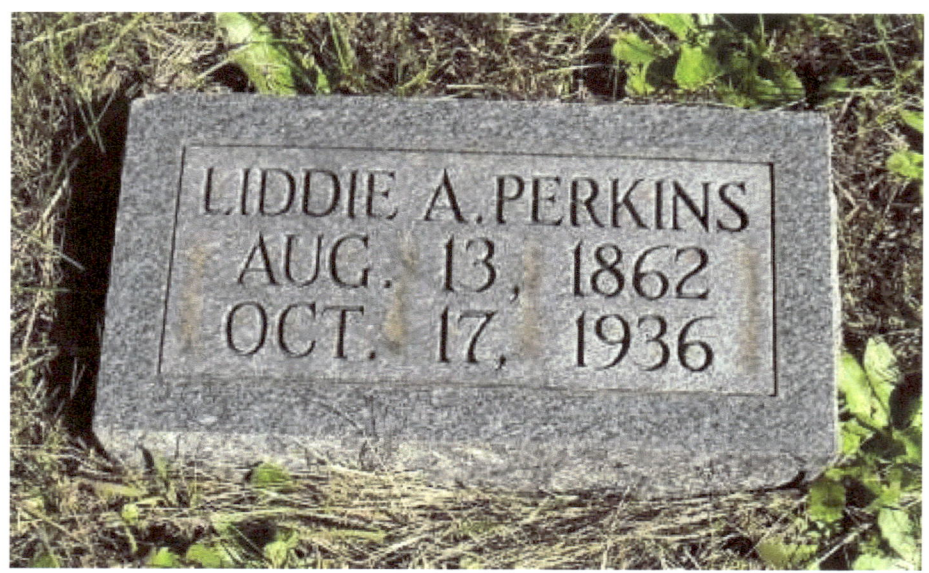

GENERATION THREE

William Green Perkins (1833-1909) and Asley (Elsie) Robertson (1834)

William Green was born in Tennessee and died in Henderson Co, TN.

Also married Sarah Jane Newman in 1887 at age 54.

Alcey Robertson's parents are Benjamin Robertson and Ellender ?

William Green Perkins gravestone

His children with Alyce:

Nancy Jane 1856-1930 married James Melvin Clenney

Mary E.   1957-1901 married Jessey Alexander Clenney

Charles Mack 1860-1936 married Lydia Hopper

Martha L. Scott   1863-

Cynthia Addoline   1864-1895

Nicie Carolina   1868-1933

Virgil   1871 -

GENERATION FOUR

William Perkins (1807-1880) and Sarah Smith (1812-)

Born in TN, moved to Clark Co, Arkansas after 1850.   died in Harrison County, Texas.

Sarah born in NC.

Their children:

William Green Perkins - 1833-1909 married Sarah J. Newman   and Alcey Robertson.

Marcella Priscilla 1835-1923 stayed in TN married a Johnson / died of Tuberculosis.

Priscilla and her children:

John D. 1837 married Nancy Jane Smith

Elizabeth C. 1839 married H.E. Roper

Addison 1841-

Nancy Catherine. 1843-1916 married William "Billy" Emmerson and married Christopher McLain (Pony) Starr . She died in Texas

Sarah 1845-1910 married John Jackson and settled in Texas

Drury Washington 1848-1828 married Mary E. "Priss" Jackson died in Texas

Isaac W. Perkins 1850-

Mary F. 1854

Martha 1856 -

WILLIAM PERKINS

William Perkins was born ca. 1807 in Tennessee, but moved from Henderson County, TN, to Clark County, AR, shortly after the 1850 Census. He and his wife, Sarah (Smith?), born ca. 1812 in North Carolina, and the following children were living in Cedar Township of Clark County as of 1860: (1) William Green Perkins was born 23 October 1833 and died 8 August 1909. He married Sarah J. Newman. William did not go to Arkansas but continued to live and died in Henderson County, TN. (2) Priscilla Perkins was born 16 December 1835 in Tennessee and died 6 November 1923 in Tennessee. She married a Johnson. Priscilla, after a son, George Johnson, was born in Arkansas, went to Texas, but returned to Hardin County, TN, in 1880. (3) John D. Perkins was born in 1837 in Tennessee. He married Nancy Jane Smith on 22 September 1857 in Clark County by Elder John Dennington. (4) Elizabeth C. Perkins was born in 1839 in Tennessee. She married H. E. Roper on 21 May 1859, in Clark County. (5) Addison Perkins was born in 1841 in Tennessee. (6) Nancy C. Perkins was born in 1845 in Tennessee. (7) Sarah Perkins was born in 1845 in Tennessee. (8) Drury W. Perkins was born in 1848 in Tennessee. (9) Isaac W. Perkins was born in 1850 in Tennessee. (10) Mary F. Perkins was born in 1854 in Tennessee. (11) Martha Perkins was born in 1856 in Tennessee.

—submitted by Ed Adams

GENERATION FIVE

Samuel Perkins (1783-1853) and Elizabeth Marsh (1785-1819) and

Mary Anna Ussery (1793-1850)

Samuel born in Anson, North Carolina and died in Hardin, TN. About 1815 Samuel moved his family from Anson Co NC to Giles Co TN and there settled as a farmer. Then in the 1830s he moved to Hardin Co TN and began farming on close to 1000 acres of land. A native of NC, of English and Scotch.   Samuel Father is Jacob Perkins b:1756 Blanden NC d: 1819 Carter Co Tn.

Elizabeth Marsh was born in Mecklenburg, Cabarrus, NC and died in Giles, TN.   Her parents are Ebenezer Marsh and Elizabeth Waddington.   This Marsh line goes back to Captain James Marsh in 1618 from Battle of Egehill,   Kent, England.

Children with Elizabeth Marsh :

Hugh M.   1803-1862 married Anna Chaires died in Mississippi

John G. 1807-1850 married Mary S. Goff / NC to Hardin, TN

William 1808-1888 married Sarah Smith

Ebenezer Marsh 1810-1895 married Elizabeth Jane Ussery/ NC to MS

Solomon Manie 1814-1889 married Marinda Carolina Houston / NC to TN

Lucinda 1816-1900 married John Lewis Fowler

He also married Mary Anna Ussery (1793-1850) and had many children:

Amanda Perkins   1821-1893 / married a Harvey Blackburn Wade

Isom Hardeman   1823-1906

Samuel Simon 1827-1912

Simeon 1833-1908

Elizabeth Ann Louisa   1835-1907

Mary Ann 1829-1907

Samuel Perkins gravestone

GENERATION SIX

Jacob Perkins (1756-1819) and Nancy Ann Graves (1761-1842)

Born in Bladen, North Carolina   and died in Washington, Tennessee.

Jacob Perkins also served several tours against the Indians after coming to Carter County (then Washington County, North Carolina). And he was married to Ann Graves by Jonathan Mulkey, a Washington County preacher while the county was still a territory of North Carolina (1790-96).

Revolutionary War Pension Application of Jacob Perkins: R8105

He lived in Washington Co, TN with 200 acres on Little Doe Creek, Watauga River.   He married Nancy Graves.   He served in the Revolutionary War under General Marion.   He also fought the Indians after coming to Carter County, TN.   He was a school teacher

Nancy Graves was born in Washington, NC and died in Carter Co, TN

Their children:

Joseph   1781 - 1844   South Carolina to Yancy Co, NC married Elizabeth ?

Samuel 1783-1853   Anson, NC to Hardin, TN married Elizabeth Marsh

Sarah   1785-1819

Amos   1787-1856 born in TN / Died Morgan, KY / married Nancy Pierce

Esther   1792-1860

Joshua   1796-1880 born in SC, died in Carter Co, TN / married Elizabeth Kite

Jacob   1798-1870 born SC / died TN / married Nancy Powell

John   1800-1850   born SC / died TN / married Nancy Cooper

Lydia   1803-1864

Kizziah Phebe   1804-1870 married John Wesly Jones / SC to Carter, TN

Susanna 1806-1880   SC to Indiana / married William Chester Miller

Here's the War Pension Application with testimony from a Benjamin Graves :

Application for Revolutionary War Pension for Jacob Perkins, Ann Perkins, widow, R8.105

State of Tennessee)County of Monroe   )

On this 12 day of May AD one thousand eight hundred and fifty-three personally appeared before me a Justice of the Peace within and for the Soundy and State afresaid Benjamin Graves.

Ages 88 years a resident of aforesaid county in the State of Tennessee who being duly sworn according tot he Law declared that he was personally acquainted with Jacob Perkins and Ann Perkins his wife in their lifetime.   My Father moved from South Carolin to the State of Tennesse when I was about 12 years of age and we was there four years before Jacob Perkins and Ann Graves my sister was married. The day I new (sic) that they was married is this my father who was not willing to the marriage and Jacob Perkins and Ann Grave my sister runaway and was married by a clergyman by the name of Mulkey and my father become uneasy and he went to see Mulkeys to see if they was married and when he came back he stated, in my presence, that Mulkey told(e) him that he married Jacob Perkins and Ann Graves and that was near about seventy two years ago to the best of my knowledge and recollection.

And Jacob Perkins told me that he served in the Revolutionary War - I lived in three miles of Jacob Perkins when he entered the service and seved out his time and was honorably discharged.   But I do not know what become of the discharge and I am well satisfied that he did serve in the Revolutionary War but I do no know how long he did serve. Jacob Perkins was a man that could be relied on for truth and verasity in his neighborhood where he lived.

Benjamon Graves (X) his m

THIS PENSION WAS DENIED

Affidavit as to marriage of Jacob Perkins and Ann Graves, and Jacob

Perkins' Revolutionary War Service. Pension was denied because of failure to prove marriage; however, given historical context it should have been allowed.

GENERATION SEVEN

William Joshua Perkins (1730-1801) and Mary Polly Black (1739-1842)

Born in Saint Georges, Baltimore County Maryland and died April 10, 1801 in Washington County, Tennessee.   Joshua lived in SC near the Pee Dee River, and moved back to NC in 1795.

Mary Polly Black was born in Essex Co, Massachusetts and died in Carter Co, TN.   She was a fair skinned Scotch woman.

Mary Black was Baptized in Beverly MA. Residence date was 24 Feb. 1740, one year old. Source: Beverly Town records. Father: Nathaniel Black b: March 18 1709-10 Beverly MA Mother: Mary Ober.

Their children:

George   1754 -1840 Liberty County, SC married Keziah Manning

Jacob 1756-1819 . Bladen Co, NC died in Carter Co, TN

Joshua   1759 born Marion County, SC, lived in Washington County, NC.   Married Mary Mixon.

> He ended up being the head of an Opelousas, St. Landry Parish, Louisiana.   He was born on the Little Pee Dee river in the same area as Gilbert Sweat.   About the year 1777 he helped **Sweat** run off with Frances Smith, wife of John Barney Taylor. They travelled the same route from South Carolina: to North Carolina to Tennessee to Big Black River, Mississippi, and finally to Louisiana about 1804. However, they sometimes did not see each other for several years at a time [Parish of St. Landry, case no.1533]. On 15 June 1837 when he was about seventy-eight years old, his three daughters filed suit in the Court of Probate of St. Landry Parish to have a curator appointed to administer his estate because he was blind and supposedly feeble. They were Mary Perkins (wife of James **Ashworth**), Sarah Perkins (wife of Jesse **Ashworth**), and Elizabeth Perkins (wife of James

Goings). He was living with his son Jordan Perkins at the time. The estate was said to contain considerable property, mainly cattle. The case was dismissed on 3 April 1840, apparently due to the death of Joshua.   These descendants of Joshua were apparently of mixed blood – Indian or Portugese.

Isaac   1758 has 100 acres in Washington County, TN on Campbell's Creek and lived in Greenville, SC.   He also lived in Buncombe County, NC.   Married Hannah Sweat.

Lewis   1762-1783

Mary   1764 Liberty, SC

Olive   1760 married Ephraim Sweat

GENERATION EIGHT

Richard Perkins II (1689-1772) and Mary Sherrill (1693-1772)

Birth: Jul. 9, 1689 / Saint Georges -   Mosquito Creek, Baltimore

Maryland, USA

Death: Aug. 5, 1772 Rowan County North Carolina, USA

Richard Perkins is first found at Mosquito Creek, in Baltimore   County in 1683. He was a cooper by trade and later listed as a planter. Thomas Lightfoot a deputy surveyor, laid out for him, December 15, 1683, a tract of land containing 100 acres called "Perkinson" (also found as Parkington), lying upon the head of a creek called "Musket Creek." He moved after 1692 to the head of Swan Creek. In 1694 he took up a tract of land on Swan Creek called "Paradise", which he sold October 18, 1695, to Robert Mason. In 1700, he was in possession of about 300 acres on the Susquehanna River, at the place called Lapidum to which he added 180 acres, all of which descended down to his three sons, and was patented to them in 1732 under the name of "Eightrupp". He may be the Richard Parkins transported to Maryland circa 1674. Richard died by April 16, 1706 when administration bond was posted by his widow Mary Perkins with William Perkins (possibly Richard's brother) and John Mills. His estate was invoiced on May 28, 1706.Source:1. Baltimore County Families, 1659-1759, by Robert W. Barnes, page 500.

Richard married Mary Sherrill , daughter of William Sherrill and Margaret Rudisil . Mary was born about 1693 in Cecil Co., MD and died after 1772 in Rowan Co., North Carolina.

MARY SHERRILL

Birth: Nov. 25, 1693, Lincoln County, North Carolina, USA

Death: Aug. 5, 1772 Lincoln County, North Carolina, USA

Mary's parents are William Sherrill from Ermington, Devon, England and Margarette Rudisil

Their children:

Richard   1713-1789   married Elizabeth Cutchen (1717)

Richard married Elizabeth Mc Cutcheon on 5 Jan 1735

Born in St. George Parish, Baltimore Co., MD. Elizabeth was born about 1717 in White Marsh Co., North Carolina. They had four children: Robert Biggin, Richard, Reuben , and Elizabeth . "He lived in the mountains of old Virginia. He was a large powerful man. He burned pitch and charcoal, and often carried a tomahawk in his belt, by which he earned the name 'Tomahawk Dick.' His ancestors came from England. He had some trouble with the Irish. He whipped thirteen of them one morning before breakfast, and afterwards a good many of them, in a drunken state, threw him out of an upstairs window in a large building and killed him." He was about 76 years old at his death on 9 July 1789 in Lincolnton, Lincoln Co. North Carolina.

Richard Perkins was born on 18 Dec 1713 in Swan Creek, St. George Parish, MD, died on 9 Jul 1789 in Lincoln Co., NC at age 75, and was buried in Emanuel Cemetery.

General Notes: His nick name was Tomahawk Dick. for his pratice of carring a tomahawk in his belt. Richard moved his family to North Carolina some time after 1754. An inquisiton held on July 11 1789 at Lincolnton, Lincoln County North Carolina by Justice John Moore Sr. the jury found that Richard Perkins at age of 76, was killed and murdered by Ezekial Polk Jr. of Mecklenburg county, North Carolina and John Hunter, son of Edward Hunter late of Lincoln county, North Carolina. On the night of the ninth of July by force and arms they assaulted Richard Perkins They violently threw him to the floor of the courthouse and then there threw him out a second story window. He was killed by the drop of over seventeen feet. The jury found Polk and Hunter had no property in Lincoln County. Richard Perkins was the the first person burried at the Old White Church Cemetery now the Emanuel Cemetery.

William   1715-1805   Maryland to died in Livingston, Kentucky

Isaac   1718-1780

Adam   1720 born in Baltimore, MD / died in Georgia

Reuben   1722

John 1723-1788   Baltimore to Burke, NC

Avariola 1726-1742   baltimore to baltimore

Moses 1726-1778   Baltimore to Wilkes, Georgia

Joshua "Jock" 1730-1801 – born in Baltimore, MD / died Carter Co, TN /

Benjamin   1732-1799   Baltimore, MD to Wilkes, Georgia

Aventin Abington   1741-1786

GENERATION NINE

Richard Perkins 1663-1706   and Mary Utie   (1667-1735)

Richard was born in Plymount, Devonshire, England to St. George's Parish, Baltimore Maryland and died in 1706 in Swan Creek, Baltimore, MD. He married Mary Utie in 1688 at age 25 in Baltimore.

Mary Utie   Birth 1667 in Mosquito Creek, Baltimore, Maryland, United States /   Death 20 Feb 1735 in St George Parish, Baltimore, Maryland, United States

The notes say he was transported to America by force by waging war against the King. He was a Quaker.

He and wife settled in 1683 on 100 acres of land on the head of Mosquito Creek in Baltimore Co., MD. Early Maryland transportation records show that Richard I arrived in Maryland in 1676. Richard and Mary settled in 1683 on 100 acres.

THE BULLETIN OF THE ORIGINAL WILKES COUNTY (vol. 3, #3) for November, 1909, claims Robert Perkins who died in Charles Co. MD in 1668 was the father of a Robert Perkins and of Richard Perkins Sr. of Baltimore CO. MD.

"8 Jul 1685. The following convicted before Chief Justice Jefferies at the Court of Oyer and Terminer for Dorset, Somerset and Devon for waging war against the King and sentenced to be transported to the Americas [sentence enrolled on 4 Feb 1691]: ... Richard Perkins ... " (PRO: C66/3339/1 & SP (Domestic) James II Vol.1 No.159). >(Source: Peter Wilson Coldham, Complete Book of Immigrants 1661-1699, Genealogical Publishing Co, 1990, Pg 525.)or there's this guy:A Richard Perkins was transported in Maryland in 1674.

Richard may have had siblings. There was a William Perkins who married Martha Miles on 3 February 1703/4 in Baltimore Co. MD; a William Perkins named in the will of James Ines of Baltimore County 4 March 1703/4; and a William Perkins who was buried 8 January 1708. There is also Joseph Perkins and his wife Mary who had children Rachel (6 January 1725), Mary (20 December 1728), and Hannah (24 May 1731).

Our Richard surveyed 100 acres called "Parkinson" at the head of Musketo Creek in Spesutia Hundred in 1683; by 1700 that land was known as "Parkington."

An early post road from Alexandria, Virginia, to Philadelphia, PA had a link running through this county by 1670, to Bush River, by ferry to Chilbury Point, near St. George's Church at Michaelsville, on to the head of Swan Creek and to a ferry. A spur extended a short distance north along the Susquehanna toward Lapidum. Another branch began near the head of Mosquito Creek, ran to the ferry at Spesutia Narrows. The Perkinses were in the area of this major road.

Richard may have had siblings.

Richard Perkins is first found at the head of Mosquito Creek, in Baltimore (now Harford) County in 1683. He was a cooper by trade and later listed as a planter. Thomas Lightfoot a deputy surveyor, laid out for him, December 15, 1683, a tract of land containing 100 acres called "Perkinson" (also found as Parkington), lying upon the head of a creek called "Musket Creek." He moved after 1692 to the head of Swan Creek. In 1694 he took up a tract of land on Swan Creek called "Paradise", which he sold October 18, 1695, to Robert Mason. In 1700, he was in possession of about 300 acres on the Susquehanna River, at the place called Lapidum to which he added 180 acres, all of which descended down to his three sons, and was patented to them in 1732 under the name of "Eightrupp". He may be the Richard Parkins transported to Maryland circa 1674. Richard died by April 16, 1706 when administration bond was posted by his widow Mary Perkins with William Perkins (possibly Richard's brother) and John Mills. His estate was invoiced on May 28, 1706.Source:1. Baltimore County Families, 1659-1759, by Robert W. Barnes, page 500.

Richard Perkins I owned pretty much all of the land that he owned jointly with William Lofton for most of his adult life. In fact, the two of them named their land "Brotherly Love," which has always implied the possibility of some sort of a brother-in-law connection. The two apparently took care of each others' children, and the children left together after their fathers died and moved down to VA, and from there to NC, where the Perkinses, Loftins, and Sherrills all intermarried.

Lofton was either the son or grandson of Leonard Loftin of Henrico Co. VA. Lofton and Perkins seem to have moved to Swan Creek, MD, at about the same time. It's not unreasonable to think that maybe Richard Perkins himself moved up from Henrico Co. with Loftin, which would probably make our Richard one of the Nicholas Perkins clan.

Their children:

William   1691-1760   Baltimore, MD to Susquehenna, Maryland

Mary   1695-1740

Elisha   1697-1741   Maryland to Orange Co, VA

> Elisha Perkins was born Swan Creek, St.George Parish, Baltimore Co. MD
>
> Elisha was in trouble for failing to record his marriage and birth of child.   He travelled back and forth from York, Pennsylvania to Baltimore.   He was indicted for stealing a horse but claimed his innocence.   He was also brought to court for abuse of his wife Margery. She sued for alimony but claimed she never married him.   She was later accused of adultery with a Christopher Holmes and various crimes of the flesh.   In a funny twist, Elisha named Christopher his executor, but he refused, so Elizabeth, Elisha's daughter became executor of his estate.   It is also known that when Christopher died, his heir was William Sherrill, a son by Margaret Sherrill.   Elisha left nothing to Margery in his will.

Sarah   1699-1699

Martha   1701

MARY UTIE

Her parents are Nathaniel Utie and Mary Elizabeth Carter.   Nathaniel is from Jamestown, VA.   His first wife May Maploft was murdered in 1665.   There is speculation that Nathaniel her husband killed her in order to marry Elizabeth Carter.   The Carter family (John Carter) was famous in history.

MORE ON COLONEL NATHANIAL UTIE

Nathaniel was born in Jamestown in 1635 and came to Maryalnd with other Puritans who were kicked out of Virginia in 1649.   Most of these men were wealthy and powerful.

Nathaniel was given an island called Spesutie from Lord Baltimore in 1658.

Records indicate he was not a nice man – in fact he was ruthless, violent and mean.   He ended up being the largest landowner in Maryland.   He was involved for 20 years in t he Anglo-Dutch wars.

Nathaniel built a house on the island called Spesutia Manor.   He married Mary Mapletoft Ward who was a widow.

Mary Mapletoft Ward Utie died in 1665 - she was *stabbed to death*. According to Maryland court records, Mary was stabbed repeatedly in the upper arm on September 30th, 1665 and died five days later on October 4th, at Spesutia Manor. According to her husband, the stabbing was done by one of their slaves, a man named Jacob. Jacob, with only the slenderest pretense of a trial, was condemned to be drawn and hanged, and this sentence was carried out in St. Mary's City a few months later.

In early 1666, Nathaniel Utie remarried, this time to Elizabeth Carter, the daughter of John Carter of Virginia. The Carters were HUGE. Huge! Elizabeth received 1/3 of her father's estate as a wedding gift, and according to John Carter's will, she would inherit the whole shebang if her brothers should die without sons. It was a very advantageous match for Utie, and that is what made people suspicious that he committed the murder.

Although obviously no one can prove anything, this seems like a classic mystery novel plot: an ambitious and ruthless man who wants power finds himself married to a woman whose family is unglamorous and lacking in money and influence. He travels frequently and has contacts among the wealthy and powerful families of Maryland and Virginia. It seems feasible that he could have either met Elizabeth Carter, or heard that she was of marriageable age, and seen the potential for a fortuitous alliance with one of Virginia's most promising families. All he has to do is rid himself of his present wife - and lucky for him, he lives on a remote island and evidently has a *lot* of nerve.

PLUS, slavery had just been legalized in Maryland in 1664. As a slaveowner, Utie was in possession of several potential murder suspects who were legally considered subhuman and could not defend themselves against any allegations he might make against them. He had no neighbors, and if one of his other slaves should happen to witness anything, well...they couldn't testify against him in court. Hmmm.

Mary Utie was buried in a family plot near Spesutia Manor, since the first church to be established near Spesutie Island wasn't built until 1671.

GENERATION TEN

Chauncey Perkins (1645-1668) and Mardi Jo Drew (1650-1663)

and Ann Margaret Foxe (1640-

Born in Shropshire, England / died in Charles Maryland

Notes:

from "Kinsfolk of the Perkins Family" by Clarence A. Perkins publ 1953

Perkins Ancestry-Origin England

The four sons of Chauncey Perkins, who were born in England and emigrated to this country in the early years of the 17th Century were Ebenezer, William, Valentine and Richard. While they were farmers, they were ambitious to become tradesmen and mechanics - one of the reasons they came - and succeeded to some extent, as it seems one became a wagon-maker, one a blacksmith, one a wood-worker, and Valentine continued as a farmer, the work he best understood.

Their children:

Richard   1663-1706 married Mary Utie

Ebenezer

William 1665-1706

Valentine

HERE IS PERKINS CEMETERY ROAD IN CARTER COUNTY, TENNESSEE

GENERATION ELEVEN

John Perkins II (1609-1686) and Elizabeth Eveleth (1635-1684)

Birth 8 Nov 1609 in Hillmorton, Warwickshire, England

Death 14 Dec 1686 in Ipswich, Essex, Massachusetts, United States

Opened first public house in Ipswich, MA. Quartermaster John Perkins, son of John and Judith Perkins, born England, 1614, died Ipswich, Massachusetts, December 14, 1686. It was he whom a band of Indians sought to kill while he was living "in a little hut on his father's island," but was forewarned of his danger by Robin, a friendly Indian. He opened the first publishing house in Ipswich, also engaged early in the fisheries, and by reason of his connection with the trainband gained the title of Quartermaster Perkins, by which he ever after was addressed. He married Elizabeth , who died 1684, having borne him nine children : John, Abraham, Jacob, Luke, Isaac, Nathaniel, Samuel, Thomas and Mary.

Their Children:

John   1636-1659

Abraham   1640-1722

Jacob 1644-1719

Chauncey 1645-1668

Luke   1649-1694

Isaac   1650-1725

Mary   1652-1727

Nathaniel   1652-1684

Samuel   1655-1700

Thomas   1657-1722

Sarah   1659-1720

GENERATION TWELVE

John Perkins I 1583-1654 and Judith Gater (1588-1654) and Joanna Pinder

Birth 21 December 1583 in Rugby, Warwickshire, England

Death 23 Sep 1654 in Ipswich, Essex County, Massachusetts, USA

Judith is Birth 1588 in Warwickshire, England

Death 26 Sep 1654 in Ipswich, Essex County, Massachusetts, USA

Her parents are Michael Gater and Isabel elizabeth Bailey

The following is from James D. True's "The Ancestry of the True Family":

John Perkins grew up in Hillmorton, England, as had at least four generations of his Perkins ancestors before him. John and Judith lived in the parish of Hillmorton where six of their children were born and baptized. On 1 December 1630, the Perkins family of father, mother, and five children (one child having died young) set sail from Bristol, England, on the ship Lion, William Peirce, Master.

After a stormy passage of 67 days, the ship arrived off Nantasket, MA, on 5 February 1630/1, and the next day sailed on to anchor at Boston, MA.

John and Judith were among the group that formed the First Church of Boston, at Charlestown, MA. John took the oath of "freeman" in Boston, MA, on 18 May 1631.

From the records of the Colony of Massachusetts Bay on 3 April 1632, "It was ordered that noe pson wtsoever shall shoote att fowle upon Pullen Poyntte or Noddles Ileland, but that sd places shalbe reserved for John Perkins to take fowle with netts." Later, on 7 November 1632, he was one of four persons, "appointed by the Court to sett downe the bounds betwixt Rocksbury and Dorchester."

John and his family had lived in Boston, MA, for about two years when they moved to Ipswich, MA, where he had been granted some 40 acres of land. He built his house near the river at the entrance to Jeffrie's neck and later received several additional grants of land.

John and his wife Judith (Gater) Perkins had seven children, all except Lydia born in Hillmorton, England:

John Perkins (probably December 1583 - circa August 1654)

  John was born in Hillmorton Parish, Warwickshire, England, probably December 1583.   He was the son of Henry Perkins and Elizabeth Sawbridge.   He was baptized in St. John the Baptist Church in Hillmorton Parish, Warks., Eng., on 23 December 1583   He married Judith Gater in Hillmorton Parish, Warks., Eng., on 9 October 1608. John immigrated in Massachusetts, in 1631. on the first trip of the Lyon. John Perkins resided in Boston, Suffolk County, Massachusetts, in 1631. This was his first residence in the New World.   John died circa August 1654 in Ipswich, Essex County, Massachusetts.

Children of John Perkins and Judith Gater:

John Perkins Junior; Quartermaster   (probably September 1609 - 14 Dec 1686) married Elizabeth.

Elizabeth Perkins   (probably March 1610/1611 - pre Sep 1670)

Mary Perkins   (probably August 1615 - 1700) married Thomas Bradbury

Anne Perkins   (probably August 1617 -) died young in England

Deacon Thomas Perkins +   (probably April 1622 - 7 May 1686) married Phoebe Gould.

Sergeant Jacob Perkins   (1624 - 29 Jan 1699)married Elizabeth Whipple and Damaris Robinson.

Lydia Perkins   (ca May 1632 - ca 1672) married Henry Bennet.

Jacob, bpt. 12 Sept. 1624; m. (1) Elizabeth Whipple; m. (2) Damaris

Robinson, widow of Nathaniel Robinson. 7. Lydia, b. in Boston, MA; bpt. at First Church, 3 June 1632; m. Henry Bennet.

GENERATION THIRTEEN

Henry Perkins (1555-1608) and Elizabeth Sawbridge (1564-1603)

   Birth 1555 in Hillmorton, Warwickshire, , England

   Death 5 Apr 1608 in Hillmorton, Warwickshire, , England

Elizabeth Sawbridge

   Birth 1564 in Hillmorton, Warwickshire, , England

   Death 1603 in Hillmorton, Warwickshire, , England

Children:

John 1583-1654

Francis   1585-1585

GENERATION FOURTEEN

Thomas Perkins Sr. and Alice Elizabeth Kebble   died in 1613.

died in 1591

    Birth in Rugby, Warwickshire, England

   Death March 1591 in Rugby, Warwickshire, England

Alice Kebble

    Birth in Rugby, Warwickshire, England

   Death 20 August 1613 in Rugby, Warwickshire, England

Thomas Perkins was the son of Henry Perkins. Thomas married Alice

Thomas and Alice's children are:

Henry Perkins, eldest son, married Elizabeth Sawbridge 29 Nov 1579 in Hillmorton, Warwick, England.

John Perkins

William Perkins

Thomas Perkins, married Mary Ward/Bate 16 Oct 1586 in Hillmorton, Warwick, England.

Francis Perkins, 1565 in Hillmorton, Warwick, England.

Luke Perkins, 1568 in Hillmorton, Warwick, England.

Isaac Perkins, 1571 in Hillmorton, Warwick, England, married 1) Alice — and 2) Alice —.

Hillmorton Church where the family is buried.

Thomas & Alice Perkins Buried under floor of this Church: Exterior shot of church. Thomas Perkins and his wife Alys/Alice de Astley Perkins and daughter Elizabeth are buried under the center isle floor of this church. Alys/Alice was born about 1475 and died abt. Oct 15, 1538. Both Thomas and Alys/Alice and Elizabeth died in Hillmorton, Warwickshire, England.

GENERATION FIFTEEN

Henry Perkins (1500-1546) and Mary Whitener (1505-1525)

Henry born and died in Hillmorton, Warwickshire, ENgland.

married Mary at Ufton Court Manor in Hillmorton

This is Ufton Court.

GENERATION SIXTEEN

THomas Perkins (1458-1528) and Alys de Astley (1461-1538)

Thomas was born and died in Hillmorton, ENgland .

Historical details of Thomas Perkins his wife Alice de Astley d. abt 1538 as reported by Paula Perkins Mortensen in description of this seventh generation on p. 3 of her book, English Origin of Six Early Colonists by the Name of Perkins 1998.

"Thomas Perkins possibly born in Hillmorton Parish. In his will dated 3 April, and proved 21 April 1528, he directs to be buried in the church of St. John the Baptist before the Rood.   His wife Alice whose will was proved 15 October 1538, also requested that she be buried there. Children born in Hillmorton Parish: Henry, Joan/Jeyn, who married Mr. Sleyter before 1538, Julian Perkins, married Thomas? Cumpton before 1538."

In a paragraph of explanation, the author goes on to describe the inside of the Hillmorton Church of St. John the Baptist that "in the side aisle, on the right facing the altar," there are "life sized effigies of Thomas and Edith de Astley...."   The Church Vicar has detailed, according to the author, that these are ancestors of Alice de Astley, wife of Thomas Perkins.   Thomas' will directed that he "'be buried in the Church...before the Rood.'"   Found on one of two marble grave stones, each "having small portraitures in brass of a man and a woman, with divers children" is an inscription: "Here lyeth Thomas Perkins and Alice and Elizabeth, Our Lord save their souls from everlasting death. Amen."

The inside of Hillmorton Church – Hillmorton, England

GENERATION SEVENTEEN

William Perkins (1430-1495) and Joanna Reed (1434-1495)

GENERATION EIGHTEEN

Thomas Perkins, Esq 1400-1478 and Ellen Tompkins (1400-1443)

Birth 1400 in Hillmorton, Warwickshire, England

Death 1478 in Ufton, Berkshire, England

Thomas was born in 1400-1420 in Madresfield, Worcestershire, England DEATH He died in Madresfield, Worcestershire, England in 1479; he was 79. LEGAL MENTION & NOTABILITY Thomas is considered to be the progenitor of the Berkshire & Nottinghamshire Perkins Families: Berkshire descending from his son John, inheritor of the Ufton estate, and Nottinghamshire descending from his son Thomas, inheritor of the family's Madresfield properties.

In the Close Roll of 1 Edward IV (1461), Thomas is first referred to as "Thomas Perkins, Esq." in a deed in which Thomas is most likely a co-trustee with "The King Maker", Earl of Warwickshire and the latter's brother John, Lord Montague. The trust received "certain manors in Hampshire, Buckinghamshire & Hertfordshire".

MARRIAGE Thomas married Ellen TOMPKINS, who was born circa 1401 in Nappend (or Nupend), Hertfordshire, England. Ellen also had a brother, John Tompkins. Her name is also spelled "Tomplins".

GENERATION NINETEEN

Lord William Perkins 1380-1451 and Margaret Collee (1380-1451)

Birth 1380 in Ufton, Berkshire, England

Death 1451 in Ufton Court, Berkshire, England

William was the son of John Perkins (or Parkyns) of Madresfield in Worcestershire, the Seneschal to Thomas Le Despenser, earl of Gloucester. He was the first of this ancient family to have arrived in Berkshire, where he became lord of the manor of Ufton Robert. From 1411, he is named in the diocesan registry as patron of that living and is styled variously Lord of Ufton, Donzell and True Patron. He lived at the old moated site in the parish. The family were not associated with Ufton Court, the manor house of Ufton Pole, until 1567 when it was purchased by the widow of William's great great grandson.

William was attached to the service of Prince Humphrey, Duke of Gloucester, as bailiff or agent. It was probably in that capacity that he was concerned in an agreement by which one William Leyre confirmed the lordship of Child's Manor in East Barsham, Norfolk, to Humphrey, Duke of Gloucester, Eleanor his wife and William Perkins Esq. For immediately afterwards, in another deed, he released his right therein to the Duke. He sealed this deed with the arms, or, a fesse dancetty between eight billets ermines. This is the first time in which the armorial bearings of the family appear. They differ from the later shield in the number of the billets, which were afterwards increased to ten. Humphrey, Duke of Gloucester, was the brother of King Henry V, and uncle and guardian to the young Henry VI during his minority. The "good Duke Humphrey," as he was called, whose disgrace and tragic death suggested to Shakespeare the lament which he puts into the mouth of Henry: "For in the shades of death I shall find joy, in life but double death, now Gloucester's dead".

William Perkins is said in the Heralds' Visitation pedigree to have been living in the year 1419, that is, during the French wars. On 29th May that year, soon after Rouen had capitulated to the English, a meeting took place at Menlau between the French Queen, accompanied by the Duke of Burgundy, and Henry V. It was to arrange conditions of peace, the most important of which was to be the marriage of the King with the French Princess Katherine of Valois. King Henry was, on that occasion, accompanied by his brother, the Duke of Gloucester, and from the special mention of the date in connection with William Perkins, it may have been that he also was present in attendance on his patron.

In 1426 and the two succeeding years, William's name appears in the accounts of the Corporation of Reading as follows: "For payment at games given before the Mayor at William Perkins', 6s. 8d. For ale given at the same, 2d. To the minstrels of the Duke of Gloucester at the Mayor's breakfast at Perkins', 20d." Whether the Mayor came out to Ufton or whether William Perkins entertained him in Reading is not clear. The Mayor had to pay for his own ale and the music and the games provided for the entertainment.

William married a lady whose Christian name was Margaret and, conjointly with her in 1424, he was party to an agreement with John Colney and Elizabeth his wife. The manor and advowson of Ufton Robert and a moiety of lands in Borwardescote were settled on the same William and Margaret and, in case of William's death, then on Margaret and her heirs male, subject to the yearly payment of eight marks of silver to Elizabeth Colney. It is certain that the manor and advowson of Ufton Robert had been already, for some years past, the property of William Perkins. This deed may, therefore, perhaps be considered as of the nature of a marriage settlement on his wife. From the fact that Elizabeth Colney had a charge on the Ufton Estate, it seems probable that she was in some way a relation of William Perkins - perhaps his own or his wife's sister. John Colney was the owner of a manor in the neighbouring parish of Padworth, called Hussey's Manor, and his name appears, with that of William Perkins, in a list of gentry of the county of Berkshire, returned in 1434 by Robert Neville, Bishop of Salisbury.

In 1427 and during several succeeding years, William Perkins served as Escheator for the counties of Berkshire and Oxfordshire. The most important event, however, in which he took part - at least, as regards the history of Berkshire - was the ecclesiastical union of the two parishes of Ufton Robert and Ufton Richard (or Nervet). In 1435, an agreement to this effect was sanctioned by the Lord Bishop of Salisbury and signed respectively by William Perkins and the Prior of the Knights of St. John of Jerusalem, who with his brethren had owned the advowson of the smaller living. This they now resigned and William Perkins and his successors henceforth, for several generations, held the patronage of the united living of Ufton as it now is.

In 1444, William signed his name as a witness to a deed of grant, made by King Henry VI, to the Provost and College of Eton, of lands in New and Old Windsor and in Clewer. In 1447, he is mentioned in the Court Rolls of the Manor of Bray as still holding the office of bailiff to the Duke of Gloucester. The manors of Bray and Cookham had been granted to the Duke by his father, Henry V.

William must have died not very long after this date, it is thought in 1449. For, two years later, his son, Thomas, presented to the living of Ufton as true patron. Around the same time, his wife gave birth to a son, who they called Humphrey after his father's old patron.

GENERATION TWENTY

John Perkins 1360-1399 and Margaret 1350-1370

    Birth 1360 in Madresfield, Worcestershire, , England

    Death 5 January 1399 in Madresfield, Worcestershire, , England

Madresfield Manor

John Perkins prospered, becoming Lord of Madresfield manor and carrying on the "family business", inheriting the position of High Steward to the DeSpencer family. In a 1398 Court Toll of Madresfield manor, he is listed as Seneschal and Amiger to Thomas DeSpencer, Earl of Gloucester.

GENERATION TWENTY-ONE

Henry Perkins (1340-1374) and Bessie Evlala Spier (1340-1399)

> Birth 1340 in Shropshire, , England

> Death 1374 in Hillmorton, Warwickshire, England

Henry Perkins was High Steward of the DeSpencer family at the estate of Hanley Castle, the fortification which guarded the forest of Malvern on the River Severn, England. the castle was surrounded by two moats, one of which remains today, as the vestige left of the castle.

Henry is the first one in the family to bear the surname variant on "Perkins". As the French influence on England waned and all things French became personal & political liabililties, Henry further modified and Anglicized his surname from "Pierrekin" to "Pierkyn".

GENERATION TWENTY-TWO

Pierre de Morlaix   (1305-1381) and Agnes taylor (1325-1360)

> Birth 1305 in Bretagne,Morlaix,Normandy,France

> Death 1381 in Shropshire,England

GENERATION TWENTY - THREE

Peter Viscount Leon DeBreatagne (1272-1312)

> Birth 1272 in Rennes, Ille-et-Vilaine, Bretagne, France

> Death 1312 in Rennes, Ille-et-Vilaine, Bretagne, Franc

GENERATION TWENTY FOUR

John II Duke of Brittany, Earl of R De Dreux 1238-1305 and Beatrix Princess of E. Plantagenet 1242-1275

John II Duke of Brittany, Earl of Richmond De Dreux

> Birth 4 January 1238 in Rennes, Ille-et-Vilaine, Bretagne, France

> Death 18 November 1305 in Lyons, Rhone, Rhone-Alpes, France

John II (in Breton Yann II, in French Jean II de Dreux) (1239 – November 18, 1305) was Duke of Brittany and Earl of Richmond, from 1286 to his death. He was son of Duke Jean I and Blanche, princess of Navarre.

On January 22, 1260, John married Princess Beatrice of England, a daughter of King Henry III of England and Eleanor of Provence. Beatrice is the daughter of King Henry III of England Plantagenet and Eleanor of Provence Berenger.

BEATRICE

Beatrice   Birth 25 June 1242 in Bordeaux, Gironde, Aquitaine, France /   Death 24 March 1275 in Bretagne, France

Beatrice was a Princess of England as the daughter of King Henry III of England and Eleanor of Provence. She was born in Bordeaux, France. Her family were members of the Royal house of Plantagenet, which first ruled in the 12th century and was founded by Henry II of England.

Beatrice and John II had seven children:

> Arthur II, Duke of Brittany

> John of Brittany, Earl of Richmond

> Marie of Brittany, Countess of Saint-Pol, wife of Guy III of Châtillon   (1268–1339)

> *Pierre, Viscount de Leon (1269–1312)*

Blanche of Brittany, wife of Philip of Artois (1271–1327)

Eleonore, Abbess of Fontevrault (1274–1329)

GENERATION TWENTY FIVE

Jean I De Bretagne (1217-1286) and Blanche DeChampagne 1222-1283

Jean I DeBretagne

Birth 1217 in Rennes, Ille-et-Vilaine, Bretagne, France

Death 8 October 1286 in Lisle, Dordogne, Aquitaine, France

They had the following children:

John II, Duke of Brittany, married Beatrice of England

Peter of Brittany, Lord of Hade

Alix of Brittany, married John of Châtillon

Theobald (1245–1256)

Theobald (died soon after birth)

Eleanor (1248)

Nicolas of Brittany (1249–1261)

Robert (1251–1259)

GENERATION TWENTY SIX

PIERS BRAINE 1188-1250 and Alice DeThouars 1201-1221

    Birth 1188 in Braine, Aisne, Picardie, France

    Death 28 May 1250 in From, Vestfold, Norway

Their Children:

Jean I de Dreux, Duc de Bretagne+ b. 1217, d. 1286

Yolande de Bretagne, Comtesse de Penthièvre et Porhoët+ 3 b. 1218, d. 1272

GENEATION TWENTY SEVEN

Robert II Count of Dreux Braine 1160-1218 and Yolande Coucil 1168-1222

    Birth 1160 in Dreux, Eure-et-Loir, Centre, France

    Death 28 December 1218 in Eure et Loire, Beauce, Centre, France

He participated in the Third Crusade, at the Siege of Acre and the Battle of Arsuf. He took part in the war in Normandy against the Angevin Kings between 1193 and 1204.

His first marriage with Mahaut of Burgundy (1150–1192) in 1178 ended with separation in 1181 and produced no children. The excuse for the annulment was consanguinity.

His second marriage to Yolande de Coucy (1164–1222) produced several children: Peter, Henry, John, Robert II, Phillipa

GENERATION TWENTY EIGHT

Robert I Count of Dreux 1123-1188 and Agnes Countess Braine de Baudemont 1130-1218

Birth 1123 in Champagne, Dordogne, Aquitaine, France

Death 11 October 1188 in Braine, Aisne, Picardie, France

HIS WIVES

1. Agnes de Garlande 1122–1143 had one child Simon

2. Hawise Salisbury 1118–1152 had children Adele and Alice

3. Agnes de Baudemont, Countess of Braine (1130 -1202)

had children: Robert II, Philippe, Isabella, Peter, Henry, William, John, Alix, Mamilie.

GENERATION TWENTY NINE

King Louis VI 1081-1137 and Adelaide DeMaurienne 1092-1154

Birth 1 December 1081 in Paris, Ile-de-France, France

Death 1 August 1137 in Paris, Paris, Ile-de-France, France

Louis VI called the Fat, was King of France from 1108 until his death 1137.   Louis was born in Paris, the son of Philip I and his first wife, Bertha of Holland.

Louis VI died on August 1, 1137, at the castle of Béthisy-Saint-Pierre, nearby Senlis and Compiègne, of dysentery caused by his excesses, which had made him obese. He was interred in Saint Denis Basilica. He was succeeded on the throne by his son Louis VII, called "the Younger," who had originally wanted to be a monk.

He married in 1104: 1) Lucienne de Rochefort — the marriage was annulled.

Their child:

Isabelle (c.1105 – before 1175), married (ca 1119) William of Vermandois, seigneur of Chaumont

He married in 1115: 2) Adélaide de Maurienne (1092–1154)

Their children:

Philip (1116 – October 13, 1131), King of France (1129–31), not to be confused with his brother of the same name; died from a fall from a horse.

Louis VII (1120 – November 18, 1180), King of France

Henry (1121–75), archbishop of Reims

Hugues (born ca 1122

Robert (ca 1123 – October 11, 1188), count of Dreux

Constance (ca 1124 – August 16, 1176), married first Eustace IV, count of Boulogne and then Raymond V of Toulouse.

Philip (1125–61), bishop of Paris. not to be confused with his elder brother.

Peter of France (ca 1125–83), married Elizabeth, lady of Courtenay

GENERATION THIRTY

Phillip I 1052-1108 and Bertha of Holland

Philip I was King of the Franks from 1060 to his death. His reign, like that of most of the early Capetians, was extraordinarily long for the time.

Philip was born 23 May 1052 at Champagne-et-Fontaine, the son of Henry I and Anne of Kiev. Unusual at the time for Western Europe, his name was of Greek origin, being bestowed upon him by his mother. Although he was crowned king at the age of seven, until age fourteen (1066) his mother acted as regent, the first queen of France ever to do so. Baldwin V of Flanders also acted as co-regent.

Philip first married Bertha in 1072.   Although the marriage produced the necessary heir, Philip fell in love with Bertrade de Montfort, the wife of Fulk IV, Count of Anjou. He repudiated Bertha (claiming she was too fat) and married Bertrade on 15 May 1092. In 1094, he was excommunicated by Hugh of Die, for the first time; after a long silence, Pope Urban II repeated the excommunication at the Council of Clermont in November 1095.– Several times the ban was lifted as Philip promised to part with Bertrade, but he always returned to her, but in 1104 Philip made a public penance and must have kept his involvement with Bertrade discreet. In France, the king was opposed by Bishop Ivo of Chartres, a famous jurist.

In 1077, he made peace with William the Conqueror, who gave up attempting the conquest of Brittany.   In 1082, Philip I expanded his demesne with the annexation of the Vexin. Then in 1100, he took control of Bourges.

Philip died in the castle of Melun and was buried per request at the monastery of Saint-Benoît-sur-Loire – and not in St Denis among his forefathers. He was succeeded by his son, Louis VI, whose succession was, however, not uncontested.

According to Abbot Suger:

"   ... King Philip daily grew feebler. For after he had abducted the Countess of Anjou, he could achieve nothing worthy of the royal dignity; consumed by desire for the lady he had seized, he gave himself up entirely to the satisfaction of his passion. So he lost interest in the affairs of state and, relaxing too much, took no care for his body, well-made and handsome though it was. The only thing that maintained the strength of the state was the fear and love felt for his son and successor. When he was almost sixty, he ceased to be king, breathing his last breath at the castle of Melun-sur-Seine, in the presence of the [future king] Louis... They carried the body in a great procession to the noble monastery of St-Benoît-sur-Loire, where King Philip wished to be buried; there are those who say they heard from his own mouth that he deliberately chose not to be buried among his royal ancestors in the church of St. Denis because he had not treated that church as well as they had, and because among so many noble kings his own tomb would not have counted for much.

Picture below is Melun Castle from an old postcard

Bertha of Holland (c. 1055 – 1093), was queen consort of the Franks from 1072 until 1092, as the first wife of King Philip I. Bertha's marriage to the king in 1072 was a result of peace negotiations between him and her stepfather, Count Robert the Frisian of Flanders. Philip, however, grew tired of his wife by 1090, and repudiated her in 1092 in order to marry the already married Bertrada of Montfort. That marriage was a scandal since both Philip and Bertrada were already married to other people, at least until Queen Bertha died the next year.

Bertha was the daughter of Count Floris I of Holland and his wife, Gertrude of Saxony. Count Floris I was assassinated in 1061, and two years later her mother remarried to Robert of Flanders. Robert, now known as Robert the Frisian, became guardian of Bertha and her six siblings.

In 1092, Philip announced his decision to divorce "the noble and virtuous daughter of Florent count of Holland and stepdaughter of Robert the Frisian" and marry the already married Bertrada of Montfort, the wife of Count Fulk IV of Anjou. The repudiated queen withdrew to the fortress of Montreuil-sur-Mer, which was part of her dower land.   By doing so, Philip infuriated his stepfather-in-law. Bertha died soon thereafter, simplifying matters for Philip who was now free to remarry – though not the Countess of Anjou, whose husband Fulk was still living.

Together, Philip and Bertha had three children:

1. Louis VI of France (1 December 1081 – 1 August 1137)

2. Constance, married Hugh I of Champagne before 1097 and then, after her divorce, to Bohemund I of Antioch in 1106

3. Henry (b. 1083) (died young)

Philip's children with Bertrade were:

4. Philip, Count of Mantes (fl. 1123)[12]

5. Fleury, Seigneur of Nangis (1093 – July 1119)[13]

6. Cecile of France

GENERATION THIRTY ONE

King Henry I (1008-1060)   and Anne of Kiev

King of the Franks from 1031 to his death.

A member of the House of Capet, Henry was born in Reims, the son of King Robert II (972–1031) and Constance of Arles (986–1034)   He was crowned King of France at the Cathedral in Reims on 14 May 1027, in the Capetian tradition, while his father still lived. He had little influence and power until he became sole ruler on his father's death.

In an early strategic move, Henry came to the rescue of his very young nephew-in-law, the newly appointed Duke William of Normandy (who would go on to become William the Conqueror), to suppress a revolt by William's vassals. In 1047, Henry secured the dukedom for William in their decisive victory over the vassals at the Battle of Val-ès-Dunes near Caen, however Henry would later support the barons against William until the former's death in 1060.

King Henry I died on 4 August 1060 in Vitry-en-Brie, France, and was interred in Basilica of St Denis. He was succeeded by his son, Philip I of France, who was 7 at the time of his death; for six years Henry's queen Anne of Kiev ruled as regent.

He was also Duke of Burgundy from 1016 to 1032, when he abdicated the duchy to his brother Robert.

Henry I was betrothed to Matilda, the daughter of Conrad II, Holy Roman Emperor, but she died prematurely in 1034. Henry then married Matilda of Frisia, but she died in 1044, following a Caesarean section. Casting further afield in search of a third wife, Henry married Anne of Kiev on 19 May 1051. They had four children:

1. Philip I (23 May 1052 – 30 July 1108)

2. Emma (born 1054, date of death unknown)

3. Robert (c. 1055 – c. 1060)

4. Hugh "the Great" of Vermandois (1057–1102)

ANNE OF KIEV

Anne of Kiev (born **Anna Yaroslavna**, also called **Agnes**; c. 1030 – 1075) was the Ruthenian queen consort of Henry I of France from 1051 to 1060, and regent for her son, Philip I of France. Her parents were Yaroslav the Wise, Grand Prince of Kiev and Novgorod, and Ingegerd Olofsdotter of Sweden, his second wife. Anne founded St. Vincent Abbey in Senlis.

Anne was born in Kiev between 1024 and 1032.

The new queen consort was not instantly attracted to her new realm. She wrote to her father that <u>Francia</u> was "a barbarous country where the houses are gloomy, the churches ugly and the customs revolting." Anna complained that the French could not read and write, and did not wash themselves. Anna of Kiev could read and write five languages, including Greek and Latin, while her husband and his entire court could not read and write, and signed themselves with a cross. At her wedding banquet, she was shocked to have only three dishes, while at her father's court in Rus', she had five dinner dishes every day. Anna could ride a horse, was knowledgeable in politics, and actively participated in governing France, especially after her husband died

For six years after Henry's death in 1060, she served as regent for Philip, who was only eight at the time. She was the first queen of France to serve as regent. Her co-regent was Count Baldwin V of Flanders. Anne was a literate woman, rare for the time, but there was some opposition to her as regent on the grounds that her mastery of French was less than fluent.

A year after the king's death, Anne, acting as regent, took a passionate fancy for Count Ralph III of Valois, a man whose political ambition encouraged him to repudiate his wife to marry Anne in 1062. Accused of adultery, Ralph's wife appealed to Pope Alexander II, who excommunicated the couple. The young king Philip forgave his mother, which was just as well, since he was to find himself in a very similar predicament in the 1090s. Ralph died in September 1074, at which time Anne returned to the French court. She died in 1075, was buried at Villiers Abbey, La Ferte-Alais, Essonne and her obits were celebrated on 5 September. All subsequent French kings were her progeny.

Children With Henry I of France:

- Philip I of France (23 May 1052 – 30 July 1108)

- Robert (c. 1055 – c. 1060)

- Emma (1055 – c. 1109)

- Hugh I, Count of Vermandois (1057 – 18 October 1102)

GENERATION THIRTY THREE

Robert II (972-1031) and

Robert II (27 March 972 – 20 July 1031), called the Pious (French: *le Pieux*) or the Wise (French: *le Sage*), was King of the Franks from 996 until his death.

Seal of Robert II
Despite his marital problems, Robert was a very devout Catholic, hence his sobriquet "the Pious." He was musically inclined, being a composer, chorister, and poet, and making his palace a place of religious seclusion, where he conducted the matins and vespers in his royal robes.

Constance gave him surviving children:

Hedwig (or Advisa), Countess of Auxerre (c. 1003 – after 1063), married Renauld I, Count of Nevers on 25 January 1016 and had issue.

Hugh Magnus, co-king (1007 – 17 September 1025)

Henry I, successor (4 May 1008 – 4 August 1060)

Adela, Countess of Contenance (1009 – 5 June 1063), married (1) Richard III of Normandy and (2) Count Baldwin V of Flanders.

Robert (1011 – 21 March 1076)

Odo or Eudes (1013–c.1056), who may have been intellectually disabled and died after his brother's failed invasion of Normandy

Constance (1014–1052), married Count Manasses de Dammartin.

Robert also left an illegitimate son: Rudolph, Bishop of Bourges.

Effigies of Robert II (middle) and Constance d'Arles (front) at Basilique Saint-Denis.

The excommunication of Robert the Pious

GENERATION THIRTHY FOUR

Hugh Capet (940-996) and Adelaide of Aquitaine

Hugh Capet was the first "King of the Franks" of the House of Capet from his election in 987 until his death.
He was born in Paris, France in 940 and also died in Paris, France.

His family were powerful landowners in France.   His family had many ties to France and Germany.   Hugh Capet was interred in the Saint Denis Basilica. His son Robert continued to reign.

The beginnings of modern France started with Hugh Capet and the Royal dynasty that followed.   This family ruled France from 987 to 1328.

Hugh Capet married Adelaide, daughter of William Towhead, Count of Poitou.

Their children are as follows:

Gisela, or Gisele, who married Hugh I, Count of Ponthieu

Hedwig, or Hathui, who married Reginar IV, Count of Hainaut

Robert II, who became king after the death of his father

GENERATION THIRTY FIVE

Hugh The Great 898-956 and Hedwig of Saxony 910-965

Hugh the Great (898 – 16 June 956) was the Duke of the Franks and Count of Paris.

He was born in Paris, Île-de-France, France. His eldest son was Hugh Capet who became King of France in 987. His family is known as the Robertians.

Hugh married first, in 922, Judith, daughter of Roger Comte du Maine & his wife Rothilde. She died childless in 925.

Hugh's second wife was Eadhild, daughter of Edward the Elder, king of the Anglo-Saxons, and sister of King Æthelstan. They married in 926 and she died in 938, childless.

Hugh's third wife was Hedwig of Saxony, daughter of Henry the Fowler and Matilda She and Hugh had:

> Beatrice married Frederick I, Duke of Upper Lorraine.[a][1]
>
> Hugh Capet.[16]
>
> Emma   (c. 943-aft. 968).[16]
>
> Otto, Duke of Burgundy, a minor in 956.[15]
>
> Odo-Henry I, Duke of Burgundy (d. 1002).[15]

Hedwige of Saxony (also *Hedwig*, *Hadwig*) (c. 910 – May 10, 965) was a member of the Ottonian dynasty and a descendant of Charlemagne. She was married to Hugh the Great. Their son, Hugh Capet was the founder of the Capetian dynasty.

Hedwig was a younger daughter of Henry I the Fowler, and his second wife Matilda.   When Hedwig's husband died in 956, her son Hugh Capet was still underage. Although Hugh inherited his father's estates, he did not rule independently from the beginning. Along with her brother, Bruno, Hedwig acted as Hugh's regent until he came of age.

Hedwig's parents are Henry the Fowler and Matilda of Ringelheim.

GENERATION THIRTY SEVEN

Robert I of France and Beatrice of Vermandois

Robert I of France (866–923) was the king of West Francia from 922 to 923.

Robert was born in 866 the posthumous son of Robert the Strong, count of Anjou, and the brother of Odo, who became king of the Western Franks in 888.

Robert was killed in the battle near Soissons in 923.

Robert's first wife was Aelis. By her he had two daughters:

> Adele of France (c. 887–aft. March 931) to Herbert II of Vermandois

Robert married secondly, c. 890, Béatrice of Vermandois, daughter of Herbert I of Vermandois. Together they had :

> Emma of France (894–935), married to Rudolph, Duke of Burgundy[10]

> Hugh the Great,(898-) who was later *dux Francorum*. Hugh was the father of Hugh Capet, King of the Franks.

Beatrice, born c. 880 was the daughter of Herbert I, Count of Vermandois. Through her marriage to Robert I, she was an ancestress of the Capetian dynasty. On 15 June 923 her husband Robert was killed at the Battle of Soissons shortly after which their son Hugh was offered the crown but refused. Beatrice died after March, 931

GENERATION THIRTY EIGHT

Robert the Strong

Robert the Strong (died 2 July 866), also known as Robert IV of Worms. His family is named after him and called the Robertians.

During the reign of Louis the German in East Francia, the Robertian family emigrated from East Francia to West Francia.

His children:

> Odo of France, King of Western Francia

Robert I of France, King of Western Francia.

GENERATION THIRTY NINE
Robert IIII of Worms 800-834 and Waldrada of Worms

Robert III (800–834), also called **Rutpert**, was the Count of Worms and Rheingau of the illustrious Frankish family called the Robertians. He was the son of Robert of Hesbaye.

He was the great-great-grandfather of Hugo Capet, the founder of the Capetian dynasty that ruled France until the French Revolution in 1792.

GENERATION FOURTY

Robert of Hesbaye died 807

Robert II, also (died about 807) was a Frankish nobleman who was count of Worms and of Rheingau and duke of Hesbaye around the year 800.

GENERATION FORTY ONE

Thuringbert of Worms and Rheingau

Turincbertus was born in 745. He was the son of Rupert I Von Haspengau of the Upper Rhine and of Wormsgau and Williswint of Wormsgau. He passed away in 770.

Birth

    Birth:

    Date: 757

    Place: Rhineland-Palatinate, Worms, Rheinland-Pfalz, Germany

Death

    Death:

    Date: 770

    Place: Worms, Rhineland, Bayern, Germany

    Place: Rhineland-Palatinate, Worms, Rheinland-Pfalz, Germany

GENERATION FORTY TWO

Rupert I Von Haspengau of the Upper Rhine and of Wormsgau and mother Williswint of Womsgau.

1st Count of Wormagau

GENERATION FORTY THREE

Lantbertus (Robertian) and Chrotlinde (De Franks) Robertian

Born 700 / died 764 in Worms, Rheinland-Pflaz Germany

Children:

Thuringbert Thurgovie

Rober 1 Cancor

Rupert THurgau

Thuringbert Robewrt Wormsgau

GENERATION FORTY FOUR

Lambert II   670 in Palatine and died 741 and Chrotlinde De Franks Robertian

GENERATION FORTY FIVE

Robert II C Robertian and Doda unknown

Born 655 in Istria, France

GENERATION FORTY SIX

Lantbertus Robertian and unknown mother

born 640 belgium   / died in Lot-et-Garonne, Aquitaine, France

Children:

Lantbertus Lambert Neustria

Leutwinus Treves

Robert II

Charibert Neustria

Chrodotrude

GENERATION FORTY SEVEN

Warinus de Poitiers (620) and Gunza Poitiers (630-677)

Born France / married in Rhineland, Germany / died in Germany

Children:

Lambert I

Lambert II hesbaye

Leudwinus

Lantbertus

Leudwinus Poitiers

GENERATION FORTY EIGHT

Bodilon de Treves

Born 600 France / died 643 France